To MIKE
Thank you for all
do for poetry and the Arts
Karla K. Morton

CONSTANT STATE
OF LEAPING

Karla K. Morton

Texas Review Press
Huntsville, Texas

Copyright © 2014 by karla k. morton
All rights reserved
Printed in the United States of America

FIRST EDITION

Requests for permission to acknowledge material from this work should be
sent to:

Permissions
Texas Review Press
English Department
Sam Houston State University
Huntsville, TX 77341-2146

Acknowledgements for *Constant State of Leaping*:
"Weeding" (*Langdon Review of the Arts*), "A Perfect Night at the Observatory"
(*Langdon Review of the Arts*), "Widowed" (*Langdon Review of the Arts*),
"You Don't Know Hot" (*Texas Poetry Calendar, Dos Gatos Press*), "Teenage,
Burning" (*Becoming Superman*), "The Making of a Hero" (*descant*), "Passing
the Gauntlet" (*descant*), "White Cherry Moon" (*Denton Record-Chronicle*),
"Old Bone Dominoes" (*Langdon Review of the Arts*), "Walking Out" (*Langdon
Review of the Arts*), "Rainbow" (*Langdon Review of the Arts*), "Twelve
Stitches" (*Texas Poetry Calendar, Dos Gatos Press*), "No Give" (*Right Hand
Pointing*), "Snow Day" (San Antonio *Poetry on the Move* Project), "Two Stars
Over Taos" (*Merging Visions. Denton Poet's Assembly*), "Eclipse" (*You Can
Have It All*, author/editor Sherry Yeary), "What Real Men Do" (*Langdon
Review of the Arts*), "Midnight on the Roof of Villa Velleron" (*Poetry Society
of Texas*), "Cyparissus" (*Ink Brush Press*), "God Bless America" (*Voices
de la Luna Journal*), "Dawn of a Nation" (*Voices de la Luna Journal*), "My
Moment of America" (*Voices de la Luna Journal*), "A Strange Peace" (*Voices
de la Luna Journal*), "A Little Flower" (*Connotations Press*).

Cover Design: "Leap of Faith" by Donna Howell-Sickles
Author Photograph: Stan Morton

Library of Congress Cataloging-in-Publication Data

morton, karla k., author.
  [Poems. Selections (Texas Review Press)]
  Constant State of Leaping / karla k. morton. ~ Edition: First.
    pages cm
  ISBN 978-1-68003-012-9 (pbk. : alk. paper)
  I. Title.
  PS3613.O77864A6 2014
  811'.6~dc23
                                2014037162

To my constant companions: John Keats, Dr. Seuss, William Stafford, Walt McDonald, Pablo Neruda, Ted Kooser, Billy Collins, Seamus Heaney, Edward Hirsch, Mary Oliver, Jane Hirshfield and Sappho, on whose wondrous words I learned to stand, and dared take up the pen.

CONTENTS

1   Weeding
3   A Perfect Night at the Observatory
4   What Real Men Do
5   Landscape
6   Tending Fires
7   Adytum
8   Two Stars Over Taos
9   Ode to an Architect
10   Cyparissus

*i. ****

13   Teenage, Burning
14   Grey Matter in Bikinis
15   Widowed
16   Happy Hunting Grounds
17   Charlie Never Let Him Go
18   A Strange Peace
19   Rebirth
20   Eclipse
21   You Don't Know Hot

*ii. ****

25   Channeling Jeremiah Smooten
29   Veronica
31   Winter in Texas
32   Your Gasp
33   Nothing But Boots
34   Letter to the Grim Reaper

iii. ***

39   The Making of a Hero
41   Passing the Gauntlet
42   Old Bone Dominoes
44   Walking Out
45   The Brown Palace

iv. ***

49   Midnight on the Roof at Villa Velleron
50   The Patron
52   Risk of Solitude
53   Salted Waters
54   Breathless
56   Good Saturday
57   Rainbow
58   Snow Day
59   Dirty Souls

v. ***

63   Contemplating the Nut
65   Whisper in the Winter
66   Letter to an Old Love
67   Diana and Apollo
68   White Cherry Moon
69   The Eternal Life of Poets
71   Overnight, the Child Becomes the Man
72   For Things That Never Lose Their Shine

vi. ***

75   The Art of the Cigarette
76   FIND AUNT FRAN'S DIAMOND EARRINGS!
78   Tiny Courtships
80   My Mother, the Seer
81   Tequila Poetry Form

82   Sin

83   Scientific Proof that Love Makes the World
       Go Round

84   Seasons

85   God Bless America

86   No Give

87   Dawn of a Nation

88   Ben Franklin

vii. ***

93   Nicole

94   God in the Bathtub

95   Twelve Stitches

96   Reference Material

97   Shameless Love Poem

98   My Moment of America

99   Pangaea

100   Paris As I See It

101   Gift Basket

102   Call Me Baby

103   Why I Married My Husband

viii. ***

107   Anniversary At Sea

108   For All Things, Great and Small

109   Her Night Eyes

110   Leap Year

112   Cattails

113   Street Corners

114   Joy

115   Legend of the Aspen: The Chrysopoeia

116   A Little Flower

Leap and the net will appear.

—John Burroughs

WEEDING

I generally avoid temptation unless I can't resist it.
—Mae West

Hunting for agates,
I found the perfect crystal
in a nest of prickly pear,

but hesitated as I reached out,
sensing him lurking,
patrolling his dangling fruit.

Weeding the flowerbed,
I sensed him *again*,
coiled in some hidden niche,

though I beat the ground,
and shook the bushes,
finally spying his curled skin,

tossed like a minute, exotic scarf.
What *kind*?
What kind doesn't matter—

I am *woman*.
He is *snake*.
Our history is tempestuous; complicated.

But I can *feel* him
like the still air before the sky breaks open;
or the pull of the witching stick

1

from the palms of my hands—
whispering *water, water.*
But he is here.

close enough to flare the tiny hairs
on my neck; the amaryllis
apple-red between us.

A PERFECT NIGHT AT THE OBSERVATORY,

learning about Big Dipper, Crow,
Orion; a flawless, cloudless
sky—a moon that just wouldn't rise . . .

and I turned to watch *you* watching
the stars—you, my Earth, my rock; *you,*
my North; my steadfast star of night.

WHAT REAL MEN DO

He was in the Core at A&M,
in the *Cavalry*,
back in 1929;
back when it was
a man's world,
and a man had to
constantly prove himself
strong and fearless.

And on Friday nights
when the moon was bright,
they would sneak out of the dorm
with their baseball bats,
and head down to the neck
of the muddy Brazos,
and club the wild gators
just for fun.

LANDSCAPE

I like the way the blue sky and Spring greens
play off each other;
and the way that painted horse has just
raised his head,
as though he heard something—
the breeze lifting his long white mane.

However, I would paint over
that *For Sale* sign and put in a little cabin—
me in a wee garden;
you, axe in hand, in a back swing
over a pile of split logs.
And we would be smiling,
since you just called out my name . . .

and the world would end
at the edge of the canvas,
our horse, forever strong;
tomatoes, ripe on the vine;
the sound of your voice, suspended
somewhere between the blue and the green.

TENDING FIRES

I wanted to write a sonnet last night,
because that's what lovers do, but the fire
needed tending, and all I could think of
were your shoulders, and *that's* not romantic,
so I put on another log, and thought
about that hot summer day underneath
that oak, when our shoulders brushed, and I
    blushed
at the nearness of you, and how we made
love that night . . . still . . . *that's* not what I wanted
to write . . . But it's you; *you,* my love. You are
my night and my morning, and the hot coals
beneath these logs . . . hear them hiss and whisper
like cicadas—cicadas of the trees,
and the summer, and of all things that burn.

ADYTUM

Michelangelo said he could stare
at a raw block of marble
and see the figure pushing to emerge.

And there is a woodsman I know
who swears he can pick up a tree branch,
and feel the throb of hawk or bowl or saint
begging for his knife.

Each man must labour for the sacred.

I yearn for the creek
to sit a while,
to learn the stillness of the trees;
the green of vines;

and soon, rocks lift their eyes;
fish rise and tumble from the water;
choruses of birds
crescendo and fall like tiny leaves;

and I begin to feel a thick holiness
looking into *my* soul.

I wonder what God sees
beneath this clamour;
this brush;
this rock hard heart.

adytum—an inner shrine; a sacred place the public is
forbidden to enter

TWO STARS OVER TAOS

They didn't just daintily *faint* from the heavens,
these stars *surged* across the night sky,

leaving a tail, like wings—brilliant and white.
I shall name them *Zena* and *Elizabeth*.

Down the road, my young cabin grows,
frame up, still open to witness such magic;

and on my dashboard, rides a tiny angel.
I shall call *her* Zena Elizabeth,

and I will tuck her inside those
unfinished walls—wood on wood—

to honour the sky, and the mountain,
and the trees that felled like shooting stars;

trees that still hover, strong and painted;
trees that curve and cradle us till dawn.

ODE TO AN ARCHITECT

for Bill Mackey

I could only do so much from afar—
lamps from a catalogue,
choosing colours from wet tree trunks
and grey doves out the window;

trusting him to create a sanctuary
from mere pen and ruler and imagination.
Yet there she is, more beautiful than I
dreamed—ten fingers, ten toes.

All night that first night, she kept us up,
creaks and shimmies and unhinged vents—
new babbles to this world;
her steady heat like warm breath.

And I, unable to stop staring, stop touching
her scraped wood, iron knuckles; the smooth
cheeks of granite. She was mine, all mine,
to tend and dress and bathe;

awed by the combination
of faith and architect;
the hum of porch swing, a lullaby
of the ever-rocking wind.

CYPARISSUS

I saw her, on the evening news,
face wrenched in pain;
her baby's death, an accident—
left in the car in the summer heat.

And my mind went back to Florence,
to a statue of Cyparissus, in *agony*,
his beloved deer, dead across
his lap, from his own bow,

just moments before Apollo
took pity on him,
turning him into a Cyprus tree
to ease his suffering.

Somehow, the human spirit survives,
their own God at the helm; a God
unwilling to let crippled hearts grow hard—
impervious in a pillar of wood.

The most dangerous thing in the world is to try to leap a chasm in two jumps.

—David Lloyd George

TEENAGE, BURNING

It was one of those combustible nights—
teenage daughter and final report cards;
seven zero's grounding her from her big
trip with friends—what she's looked forward to
    all year.

Doors slammed; words, like grenades, she'll only
regret when *she* is 45, when her
own daughter discovers matches. Times like
these we doubt we're qualified for this gig—

it would be so easy to give in, to
give her everything she ever wanted.
Tough love doesn't *begin* to describe it.
Call it *scorching*—passion burning every

exposed heart; my great love for her, groping
for answers while the house is on fire. I
sit on the floor, outside her bedroom door,
listening to her cry herself to sleep.

GREY MATTER IN BIKINIS

I have a pen addiction—
always, *always*, I'm in need of one,
yet they are *nowhere*
and *everywhere*
in my house.

Oh, the urgency
to pick one up,
grab an envelope or receipt
or blank book page
to write something down;

something that cannot wait;
something . . . *leaping.*

My pens, my thin, delicate friends—
first responders
traveling from desk to bath to purse
to kitchen to head to desk,

anticipating words—
lined up like summer divers
on the high board.

Thoughts have come,
quickly, quickly one is there—
nib out,
ready to guide them
safely to the page—

that huddled, giggling,
grey matter in bikinis.

WIDOWED

*for Georgia Calloway, and inspired by the watercolor
by Denton artist, Jo Williams
(a Spenserian Sonnet)*

*It's said only one in 10,000 acorns becomes a tree.
I think the odds are the same for finding true love . . .*

I have known a great love of oak and leaf
who held my heart strong, as winds whipped
    and twirled
around us; a love beyond my belief
that such a thing could exist in this world.

One in ten thousand finds perfection—curled
in quiet niches in the earth, in dark
pockets where moonlit rain falls hushed and
    pearled,
opening love's acorn of green and bark.

Yet, you did, my love, *you* were the one marked
by God upon my eyes, the one my soul
cannot live without, *you*, my rainbow's arc,
the only person who could make me whole.

We are seed and limb; nest and dove. I'm *left* . . .
empty without you around me, my love.

HAPPY HUNTING GROUNDS

for my father, Pete Martin

if I stand, starry-eyed, that's a danger of paradise
                                    —Tony Bennett

May you only feel joy now,
like Christmas morning,
or candles on a cake;
your soul,
stretched open and wise.

You, who have crossed over—
you now, that stranger
in paradise.

May your voice never tremble
in the thunder of your chest;
may strength swell
in a new body; new eyes;
gravity releasing all ties;

your life full of wonder
like that dawn in '71
when you startled
a flock of doves,

forgetting your gun,
watching them rise like angels
to the skies.

CHARLIE NEVER LET HIM GO

"I just don't understand how you aren't surprised,"
he said, after his favourite uncle's funeral.
"I am, and I've known him my whole life."

His namesake died in an alcoholic suicide—
crashing his car into the VA's office;
the prostitute still waiting in the dark hotel room.

'It's because you've known him your whole life,'
she wanted to say.
'How could you see anything unusual?

You grew up with him vanishing every few hours;
with his eyes always clouding at the mention of
        Vietnam.
You were too close to notice the way he entered
        every room—

the way he slowly twisted the knob,
then hesitated . . .
before opening every door.'

A STRANGE PEACE

In a million years we'll ooze from vaults and
metal caskets, back in the mud where we belong.
          —Walt McDonald, *"Praying for Rain on the Plains"*

Ship ribs stood from the mud,
unearthed in tragedy
20 feet beneath Manhattan streets,

sunk when America was just a babe;
remnants of Caribbean marine life
bored into the wood;

200 years of building, of progress;
of fire and murder and heartbreak;
yet it held strong in all the chaos,

hull intact;
a new compass point of our lives—
ground zero for the strength of a people;

a strange peace that all is well,
that hope was always there,
buried deep in the dark of the mud.

After hearing the news report of an old ship found
beneath the ruins of 9-11.

REBIRTH

I watched myself in the mirror,
draped in black plastic,
wet hair rolling up
at my shoulders—
hair twisted and fried
from chemotherapy,

and remembered my kids'
first haircut—tearing up
as those sweet curls dropped
like gold petals to the floor—
closing the last chapter
of their journey through the womb.

This, too, my first cut
in two years,
remnants from the front line
falling away in dark chainmail—
my tears, this time,
of praise and relief.

I stood, pulled off the black cape,
ran my fingers through
the new silk of hair,
and walked away;
a scatter of curls
like tiny c's about the floor.

ECLIPSE

I remember the fear,
unable to understand the big picture,
the darkness—long sober nights
zipped coffin tight around my body.

And in those months—
those deep, heavy months,
I learned to stop struggling
to find answers to questions
too immense for humanity;

and closed my eyes,
and felt a golden pinprick of light
welling up inside—
smaller than those holes we punched
in papers

in the 5th grade,
during solar eclipses;
never once doubting a teacher
who made magic from Science and God;
who taught us to witness

that unseen beast of Sun
in full form on the sidewalk;
holding its greatness in our hands;
believing sometimes, a tiny light,
is all we're ever meant to see.

YOU DON'T KNOW HOT

until you've seen August
in Texas,

her full skirt, flaring
as she settles in,
knotting her hair each night
in a low, golden ball;

laying back, stretching long
legs of sky

eastward; pink toenails
of clouds. Cowboys stop
and stare, Stetsons pushed back,
falling in love *again*;

slow exhales of *whistle*
from their lips.

When in doubt, make a fool of yourself. There is a microscopically thin line between being brilliantly creative and acting like the most gigantic idiot on earth. So what the hell, leap.

—Cynthia Heimel

CHANNELING JEREMIAH SMOOTEN

I
Introductions

She was easy to find,
mind out wandering,

two lit candles to guide
her back home.

We can see you, you know;
we who have left the earth

can spot clairvoyance a mile away
so I merely stopped in,

felt the foggy edges of her mind,
and found an open door.

II
Pros and Con with Self

All our issues are really the same, you know.
He's in bed alone because he said
my snore changed from freight train
to small animals dying,

So I wait for sleep to find him.
It seems the nice thing to do,
but it isn't; I don't want to be in there,
our time alone a heartbreak; a chore.

And when I think about leaving,
I think about
his world and mine,
who will get the lake house,

or how I will pay rent,
or how happy the neighbor will be
now that he's single.
Not once have I worried if my heart

will break; or how I will eat alone,
maybe even an early dinner—
sometimes right in the middle
of the bed.

III
Transvestites Make Me Happy

I don't know why they confuse you,
it makes perfect sense to me—
god, *finally* a woman I can lust over!

See those curves, those thick wrists;
that black inch-worm of eyelash;
those over-red lips!

It's funny, women always asked me
to be someone I'm not,
but this man, dressed like woman

is somehow authentic;
somehow without guise;
my hero in 3 inch sling-backs;
courageous,
outrageous,
alive.

IV
Dancing

It's interesting
when we all get together,
who will take the lead,
and who will choose to
be led—backwards; blind.

V
Childhood

Mother always tried to understand,
Father refused.

Mother always said the wrong thing,
Father said nothing.

Mother wondered if something she'd done
hurt me, or turned me against women,

Father only wondered
if he should have used his belt.

VI
Still a Cowboy

I can tell you I love this state;
that everything I do
pours into Her
like well water to the cracked earth.

I can tell you when I ride the range,
and tighten the fences,

I'm thinking only of brazen bulls,
and the swagger of utters.

I can tell you when I get back at night,
I don't want any of you in the bunkhouse,
and I lie on my bed, hat over my face;
praying to be something I'm not.

VII
A Trust Issue

Some people you can never confide in,
though they say all the right things.
Sometimes, you look into their eyes,
and all you can see is a far off thought—
something they choose not to say—
odd words winding a path
never meant for your feet.

VIII
I Can Tell You

I can tell you,
I am not a gay man trapped in a woman's body,
and if I was,
wouldn't that just make me *more* attracted to you?

No, I'm just a voice she heard one Wednesday;
when the moon was waning;
when she sat in the bathtub,
full and hot;

the rest of the house—
bedded hard
from the whiskey and coke.

VERONICA

a movement bullfighters do with their red capes to
encourage a charging bull. It's taken from St. Veronica,
who is always shown holding a veil in two hands like
a matador's cape. The myth is that a woman named
Veronica wiped Jesus' face on her veil, and that veil
forever held His image. It's believed now, that an
unknown woman wiped His face, and St. Veronica
never existed—the vision on the veil was called ver
(true) icon *(image)*—veronica. *Stories and time filled*
in the gaps.

Because I could not spend the day with you,
I slipped away to this safe cafe—
not too public; not too intimate,
and eavesdropped on the conversations around me,

comforted by female chatter;
the tink of spoons to dishes; kitchen noises.

Come gather the women;
the softened bodies;
the graying hair; the books, the quiche;
a red napkin in each lap.

It's an interesting thing—
our lives with men;
our lives without men.

Because I could not spend the day with you,
these places become arenas
of cool, feminine moons

who realize
men are like the sun—

bright bulls of light
who pace the floors, and fade the chairs;
who burst through our lives
all heat and horn,

and we advance and tend,
evade and retreat—
and shimmy the red capes of our skirts
to woo them from their *querencia* . . .

Come gather the men—
the hungry, the fearless, the wounded.

"*Toro, Toro*" tease the rounded women.
Into the myth, burn the men.

*querencia—area of the ring chosen by the bull where it
feels secure

WINTER IN TEXAS

Every season boasts its beauty,
but I love it *now*,
leaves raked and bagged and blown;
trees, stripped of blonde,
without pretense,
elegant in their stark brunette stance—
nests, like secret hairpins.

It's the time of revelations;
contemplations of simplicity—
a room, a lamp, a chair;
stew on the stove;
nests built one twig at a time
to cradle hearts, tiny and warm.

YOUR GASP

There was that day I came to you
unannounced
and pulled you to your room
and climbed on top of you as I pushed
you down in the sheets

and while on my knees
heaved my blouse over my head

and heard your gasp
and watched your eyes
burn across me like firelight.

I would have married you right then,
at that very moment,
had you only asked—
damn the world,
its rules;
the ticking clock beside the bed.

NOTHING BUT BOOTS

Donning her new
cowboy boots,
she rushed in to model
the hand-tooled hide—
the swirl of design;
the green laurel wreath
around a raised Texas star;
not knowing excitement
flushed her cheeks
and set her eyes on fire.
Later, still prone
upon the dining room table,
his fingers outlined
the edge of leather
around her legs—
the rise of shaft
like the swell of hearts
against her skin.

LETTER TO THE GRIM REAPER

for Mike Semler

Seriously?
Is *this* what we should expect?

Sneaking into the night
without knocking;
barging in the bedroom
while we sleep?

Dishes are piled in the sink.
The yard is two weeks past mowing.
The electric bill has yet to be paid.

For God's sake, he was only 50 . . .

Can you at least give us
a little warning—
a wee headache before the aneurism;
a few arm pains before the heart attack

that we may straighten up a bit,
toss the vibrators,
clean out the medicine cabinet,
burn the old love letters.

Ladies and Gentlemen,
this is your life—or rather the end of it.

Mr. Reaper does not care about
what's in the oven,
or the wet clothes in the washer;

his pocket watch says *now*.
Now.

Let us, collectively, turn off the porn,
and water the plants,
and fill up the cat's bowl
before we lay down to sleep.

Half the failures in life arise from pulling in one's horse as he is leaping.

—August Hare

THE MAKING OF A HERO

with love for Stephen Malley

It is surmounting difficulties that makes heroes.
—Louis Pasteur (French Chemist
and Microbiologist)

*When you get a little older, you'll see how easy it is
to become lured by the female species.*
—Batman (to Robin)

I met him on the steps of Willie Pigg Auditorium—
this boy, this beautiful boy, three years older, Adonis
dark and tall, amazed that he was looking at *me*.

The next day, a note passed through his younger
brother, and we were fast in the current of first love,
clinging to each other till I packed up for college;

leaving him to his career—a fledgling fireman.
Home for Spring Break, standing in the frame
of his new house, he spoke of his bank note,

and 50 years tumbled in my brain like barrels
down a waterfall. I watched him talk, excitement
darting his long legs room to phantom room,

this boy, this beautiful boy, so ready for honeymoons
and mortgages; the beams between us, an instant
log jam; knowledge ascending upon me like a sudden

serpent . . . and everything changed. I became his
femme fatale—the one who'd cause him to dare fate;

to charge deep into the flames; his bittersweet
   catalyst

from human to hero. Standing on the concrete
   foundation,
I took him to my breast, crying in our moment
   of sweetness,
knowing one day too soon, I would break his
   beautiful heart.

PASSING THE GAUNTLET

He never learned the language of love,
having grown up in silence at the supper table;

their only interaction, the names and scores
and stats of players and teams.

It's what he knew; what his father knew.
But on Sunday afternoons, they'd take to the yard,

two well-rubbed leathers, soft and tended and
    creased;
that baseball, bridging glove to glove; binding

father to son. Their arms, the air, the *catch*
saying everything they needed to say.

OLD BONE DOMINOES

Driving through
my old hometown
feeling it as I did
so long ago
invisible memories
standing strong
one after another
after another
stretched in a
long domino chain
just waiting for that one
renegade thought
to trip them into motion
and as I drive through
these worn spotted recollections
they topple my senses
with past emotions
and electric currents
as though I were
passing through
old ivory ghosts
lined up in a row
along the snaking
asphalt road home
home
coming home
sweet tea
chain-link fences
and the clacking
Friday night lullaby
of old bones
against

CONSTANT STATE OF LEAPING

a wooden kitchen table
shuffling yet another round
of *42*.

*"*Texas 42*", or just *"42"*, is a trick-taking domino game
created in 1887 in Trappe Springs (now Garner, Texas) by
12-year-old William Thomas and 14-year-old Walter Earl
. . . two boys who, because of their strict Southern Baptist
upbringing, were not allowed to play cards.
—*"42"* is often called the "National Game of Texas" and is
still a favourite game of many Texas grandparents today.

WALKING OUT

A man of technical precision,
he taught himself electronics—
each fascinating detail

of gears and volt meters;
the secret workings of everything
from toasters to helicopters.

But one day, a trench dug,
pieces of sprinkler system strewn
about the yard, he felt his gift

pack up the sterling of his mind
and walk out,
like an ungrateful vagrant.

I went to see him today,
every one of his clocks, haphazardly
chiming at odd times; five years of

remote controls, face down on the table,
backs off . . . two simple batteries,
helpless in his hands.

THE BROWN PALACE HOTEL

Denver, Colorado

I think, if some things
survive long enough,
and have been loved long enough,
they become *living* things.

There's a flint arrowhead
in my purse
that I have touched every day
for six years;

or my pen carved from shed antlers
of the mule deer;
or the walls of old cathedrals;
or this place—the Brown Palace—

warmth breathing from onyx walls;
sunlight sinking down through
swirled stained glass.
Even the dead linger here,

peering over iron rails—
white gloves and a pink dress.
Oh, what would such a Grande Dame
do without her people?

She is alive in starburst lamps;
restless at night in the silence;
needing the living to keep her young;
the purr of conversation—
the rush inside steel veins.

A wounded deer leaps the highest.
—Emily Dickinson

MIDNIGHT ON THE ROOF
AT VILLA VELLERON

There would have been no lights in the 14th century,
but these walls were here—some fellow crazed poet

out on this very same ledge, succulents hedged
    between
terracotta tiles; lumber at least 500 years old when

it was cut and scrolled for beams and olive presses.
He would have lived with a found cat named Chaz;

drank wine from vines planted by ancient Greeks—
as I do, glass in hand, seeking solace from these
    empty,

smooth-trod streets; the dark Luberon Mountains,
a sleeping god; the same virgin moon in our eyes . . .

counting these bells that *always* cry twice—once
    for the lovers
of the shadows; once again, for the lovers of the pen.

THE PATRON

for Marsha Dowler, Karen Holland, Jane Crew, Cathy
Toole, Robert Davis, and the entire Escape to Create
Staff, Seaside Florida

Yes, this is the wrap that got caught in my bicycle
    chains;
the one wrenched in steel and grease and rust;
the one we thought ruined and useless;
but see how it warms and glows around me.

There is a woman I know
who raised her children on her own;
who rescues the unwanted, the defeated;
who feeds the hungry—

all beings who, in turn,
watch over *her*; keep *her* safe in the night;
the sentinels of her sleeping eyes.

And she brings in artists from this cold world
to keep and nurture,
that they might turn their powers into art;
into creations that can only come
when the body is safe, and sleep is secured—
creations that engulf the world in beauty.

I wore this wrap in Florence.
It brushed the walls of El Duomo;
wiped my tears in the Uffizi as I stood helpless
before Botticelli's Pallas and the Centaur.
She helped me gently dip and clean it,
and wash it again; and lay it to heal
in the winter sun.

Some people wonder what their gifts are
in this world; people who walk about day to day
stretching their hearts to embrace
every living thing.

Perhaps these are the greatest of *all* the artists—
those that keep the fires blazing;
and an extra pillow, and a pot of beans ready;
those who take the wild, the strayed,
the broken,
and bring them, once more, into love.

RISK OF SOLITUDE

We tend to categorize poets as introverts,
though a few are boisterous and outgoing,
and some like moonflowers,
only coming out in the soft veil of night,
closing up at any bright bristle.

But most prefer to keep to themselves,
though I try to coax them with invitation
and banter and outstretched hands
but I *do* understand—

humanity is a fickle woman
who bleeds without warning.
The trees and the stars and the lizards
have never *once* let us down.

And I think of my mother, my soulful mother;
my father failing,
their lives *always* their own—
their sanctuary transformed to an island;
and I on the other side,
reaching out to only air.

SALTED WATERS

No, I did not rest well.
Words kept tossing me
to-and-fro;
slapping the hollow hull of sleep.

It was though I heard Earth murmur
through smog and diesel fumes,
and oil-slicked pelicans,
and the gouged-out eyes of the puppy
from last night's news.

It's getting harder to champion humanity.

And I thought of Key West—
my old retreat—
before the vice of cruise ships,
when the waters rolled cerulean
to tiffany to bondi blue.

Last night, I thrashed side to side
in the dark
because evil exists;
because men always mean well
in their destruction;
because the rain felt more like *weeping,*

and woke with a yearning
for salted air and coffee;
for that thin ley line
between sky and sea;
for a zen of blues;
nights when sleep
is deep and sweet.

BREATHLESS

To all you men
who love women with curves—
thank you.

Thank you for calling us sexy
when you *aren't* having sex.
Thank you for the winks and whistles
and trucker horns.

Those poor supermodel hips
couldn't bear a boy,
three times his year's weight
(starting high school football
in the eighth grade).

She couldn't handle
your smoked ribs,
or date night at the hockey game—
foot-longs with jalapenos,
and a Coors Light
every third pass of the beer vendor.

Maybe we were built to be
your comfort in winter's dark;
breasts that buoy in the lake;
that warm you in bed.

Thank you for liking
our amplified cleavage—
with and without a bra.

Thank you for pulling us close;
for making love sober,
in the daylight;

for coming up behind us
as we scowl in the mirror,
and kiss our neck, and tell us
our beauty
leaves you breathless.

GOOD SATURDAY

The risk of having children
—Walt McDonald

In a hospital bed, tubes spiking out of his head,
he reached for me, crying;
though I couldn't pick him up as they tended

to him . . . my love; my child who almost died.
Nobody ever talks about Good Saturday, though
there was nothing *good* about it for Jesus, or
    Mary—

she probably didn't even get out of bed,
succumbing to exhaustion from the night before,
to see her child, her tender, gentle child,

mocked and beaten and nailed and crucified;
holding His lifeless body in her lap.
And, oh, in those hours, those long, horrible

hours, did He look down, the boy in Him searching
for her face; whispering in his pain
. . . *Mom* . . .

Oh, the great *risk of having children!*
A child in desperate need
yet we're powerless to help;

unable to do anything
but touch his bare foot,
and call out the magic of his name.

RAINBOW

> *. . . and we'd talk to ourselves, our mouths full of*
> *spit and yearning, hoping something would give us*
> *the courage to sit in that leaping saddle, to give us*
> *the chance to fly, to listen closely as we held on tight.*
> —Alan Birkelbach, "Tommy, the
> Man Who Broke Horses"

In that final PET Scan, as slivers of light arced
about my body, I heard the voice of God—clear
and unmistakable as running water: "*This*
is my rainbow to you."

In the Dairy Queen in Dalhart, an old cowboy
talked about his horse, in that moment just after
the buck, when its body arches, and all four hooves
point downward, to the ground.

There was an odd truth in the voices—a *promise*;
an acceptance of screaming storm and fury; yet
a *belief* that we'll know the calm of earth once
        more—
patient, steady and still.

SNOW DAY

School Is Closed Due to Inclement Weather

How lucky are we, trapped in this frigid snow globe;
an unexpected birthday of ice with white bows;

a gift of time, wrapped tight
like twilight's newspaper—rolled and white;
waiting somewhere on the lawn.

DIRTY SOULS

No matter where we travel
in this life,
it seems a little mud
from *where we've been*
clings to the soles of our shoes,
mixing who we were
with who we will become.

We can only hope our human souls
get just as dirty.

The artist never entirely knows. We guess. We may be wrong, but we take leap after leap in the dark.

—Agnes De Mille

CONTEMPLATING THE NUT

Totally disgusted at the funeral home's
used car salesman techniques,
my father decided to shop around for bargains,
finding an irresistible "deal" at Caskets 'R' Us.

A deal so good, he wanted two—
one for Grandma's immediate use,
and one for him,
to wait for years
in his garage, lid open,
disguised as a planter box.

Centuries ago, Italian nuns carried
all their earthly possessions in a trunk
at the end of their bed,
and when they died, it became their coffin.

I rather like that idea—
using such beloved lumber—
touched and worn smooth over the years;

lying down inside when it's your time,
a pillow under your head, maybe one between
your knees, skin against real wood—
plain pine or oak;

then buried beneath a walnut tree;
knowing those roots would stretch down
to sup whatever nourishment they needed;
pulling you up into their limbs

to feel the tiptoe of the beetle,
the clawed fist of the crow;

pushed into tiny balls at the end of the branches
to well up as walnuts;

falling at the feet of one who picks you up,
holds your wooden world in his hands,
contemplating softened edges;
the sweet stillness curled inside.

WHISPER IN THE WINTER

Whisper in the winter
when clouds hang low and gray,
for Mother Earth sleeps sweetly
in her icy negligee.

Disturb her not with shovels—
don't insist that she awake—
for even rain has hushed its touch
with each tranquilized snowflake.

When the last leaves fell
Earth breathed a sigh,
curled up, and closed her eyes,
and slid to peaceful slumber
while the wind sang lullabies.

Whisper in the winter
her night is cold and deep.

Whisper in the winter
women need their beauty sleep.

LETTER TO AN OLD LOVE

I saw you at your mother's funeral.
I'm so sorry—
I adored her.

I wanted to tell you
you look good;
you've grown into a handsome man
from that boy I knew so long ago.

I couldn't help but stare.
Your children have your eyes.

I learned the North Star
isn't due North anymore—
the moving poles
and earthquakes
throwing the world off its axis;

like 30 years ago,
when one word shifted the universe.
I swear the earth trembled
as I walked away;
the night sky
never quite the same.

DIANA AND APOLLO

For 1,934 years, they stood,
the protectors of Pompeii,
Vesuvius in the background;

remembering their people
as they succumbed, one by one—
the sitting boy, head in his hands,

the dog, writhing in pain
at the end of his chain;
the husband, trying to shield

his pregnant wife's face, while pumice
and poisonous fumes fell from the sky,
300 degree ash climbed 23 feet,

and their cries finally stilled . . .
For 1,934 years, they've faced each other
in the barren temple built just for them;

their unmoving statues staring eye to eye;
horror bronzed in their throats: "Oh Destiny,
the great father of Zeus . . . *what have we done.*"

WHITE CHERRY MOON

for Debra Davis

Is she still reeling?
Was an angel in the passenger seat?
Did a great shaft of light lead her up to heaven?

She knows *everything now*—
JFK's conspiracy truth,
the Marfa Light mystery,
the colour of God's eyes.

And we are here,
tossed in the wake of her passing,
her ferocious soul, zooming up ahead.
Does she know we think of her?

Let us toast this vivid woman,
stepping out—her body, an overcoat,
puddling to the earth, her freed spirit,
drifting wherever she pleases.

On this, the longest night of our lives,
as death eclipses our hearts, let us raise a glass,
brimming dark with winter solstice—
the full moon, a big white cherry.

Be well, my friend;
swallow the light;
each day now, leading only to Spring.

—21Dec10: Winter Solstice, full moon, total lunar eclipse,
and the death of my friend

THE ETERNAL LIFE OF POETS

I do not know, dear reader, what year this will
    reach you,
but it's 2012 here, heavy with July's heat,

and I am lying on a sailboat
beneath a Night so moonless and clear,
the stars glisten on Her black velvet corset.

Time has no meaning to the stars.
It's taken some of them hundreds of years to
    reach our eyes—
beginning their journey when Sappho and Dante
    and Shelley
and all those names unknown were alive
pen in hand like me.

Know, dear reader, that I lived, and I loved—
Oh God, how I loved!
Earth steadied my feet above her head;
the wind carried my breath;
rivers offered my pale belly,
like a babe, to the sun.

We are thick, now, with people;
light pollution smokes the heavens;
but every once in a while, like tonight,
the old magic shines through.

I wish this for you, my friends—
a soul-filling simplicity;
slow days upon the water;
a circle of old waning friends;

a chance to gaze upon the perfect,
exquisite body of Night.

And when you feel a little lonely,
I'll be here in some ancient book;
waiting for you to look up, and open your palms;
my words, a white-hot burning
across the dark torso of time.

OVERNIGHT, THE CHILD BECOMES THE MAN

Ekphrastic poem inspired by artist Jon Hawkin's painting titled "Leaping Sheep"

Flying into the night sky—
into the magic
of moonlit clouds;
woolen billows
and rounded humps
in a constant state of leaping

This is what dreams are made of—
of wandering like a lamb
through the floating white abyss
of childhood,
then suddenly emerging
into self;
into consciousness;
into the brilliant, clear sunrise

of a world waiting below,
fortified with the strength of age;
with the hungry, searching soul
of a hawk

FOR THINGS THAT NEVER LOSE THEIR SHINE

There is pleasure in things that stay ready—
the walking stick against the doorframe;
sharpened pencils on a pad;

keys on the hook;
a bowl of grapes;
music loaded and ready.

And in my closet, I pull out
a brand new pair
of black patent leather heels;

the other shoes jealous of their shine;
the new girls on the block
catching the boys by the groin.

The hickory standing a little taller;
hourglass sketches on paper;
keys rattling;
grapes, softening to wine;

and the record drops
to the hiss and scratch of Sinatra,
One for My Baby, and One More for the Road . . .

I've decided life is too fragile to finish a book I dislike just because it cost $16.95 and everyone else loved it. Or eat a fried egg with a broken yolk (which I hate) when the dog would leap over the St. Louis Arch for it.

—Erma Bombeck

THE ART OF THE CIGARETTE

It isn't so much about the cigarette;
it's about herbs, crushed and lit;
smoke streaming about the head
like cold mountain mornings;
a warm habit—hand to hand;
lip to lip.

It's about *time*—
a purple curl of plum, plucked from the day;
a step out into the air, the sun;
one shoulder up against the building—
to light that fire, and rest the mind.

It's about evening,
when chores are done,
the kids, put to bed.
It's a whiskey over ice, sweetened with coke;
conversations between crickets;
moonlight in the eyes.

Bring *back* the cigarette;
the cigar; the pipe;
bring back the woman
in long black gloves,
red lipstick inked around
rolled white papers.

Bring back the man
tanned by the sun;
his lips, hinting of tobacco;
the wind always reaching
for his hair.

FIND AUNT FRAN'S DIAMOND EARRINGS!

She tells the story, and I'm horrified—
one pair—her only jewels—
the *one pair* of diamond earrings
she kept in her room is gone;
her things rifled through in the nursing home
when she wheeled down to dinner, or slept.

I rant, call for a lineup, employee interrogation;
remembering my in-law's neighbour when *she*
        checked in—
crying as she unclipped her earrings,
forced off her mother's rings,
pulled long strands of stone over silver bouffant,
her daughter's hands outstretched and waiting.

Hell hath no jewelry.
My jewels—my old friends, daily companions
to the grocery,
neighbour's dinner parties,
my son's graduation, my father's funeral;

charm bracelets with every silver memory of travel;
pearls that hold my warmth; anniversary gold;
the sacred mountain of turquoise at my neck,
my wrists, my fingers.

Rather I would swallow them—safely tucked in
        upper colons
than to watch them disappear—
my art, my treasures, my babes—
each one absorbing every emotion
from every day of my life—

even the ones too painful to wear—
like Kwan Yin,
last worn five years ago and counting;
brown topaz
below perfectly carved jade—
ever green with the doctor's words;
her many arms—an exquisite still life;
a perfect dance of pain.

TINY COURTSHIPS

I have lost my rush;
hurry sinking into the sand
like water.

I have watched the sun set
for three weeks; let myself
be rescued by handsome men.

Father once told me
chivalry was actually a gift
women give to *men*—
letting men use their God-given strengths
of muscle and protection.

He said it honours a man
when you wait for him,
when you let him carry your load.

For 43 years, my mother gently stood
by the door for him,
let him pull her chair at the table,

let him carry the awkward, the heavy,
let him rush fist-first into every volatile situation
while she stood back
to enter, to sit, to take, to nurse.

I have come back to the sea
after the plunging of youth,
to remember the sweet slowing—

the physical sensations
of lighting candles, and turning records,
and conversation;

the tiny courtships of women and men
like the pull and pulse of waves;

my hand wrapped tight in his;
our pockets full of shells.

MY MOTHER, THE SEER

Flying low over the earth,
I itch to be a goddess
bending down to run my hands across
the patterns of fields;
the patches of trees
like the raised paisley crewel-work
of grandma's sofa pillows.

And I am 10 years old again,
Saturday mornings with Mother
at the fabric store,
twirling in my full circle skirt
as she pores over pattern books
of pony-tailed models with tiny belted waists.

Then she'd rise, *finally*, moving past
the thread, the bobbins, the kiosks of buttons;
to the forest of wound cotton, knits and corduroys.

I'd follow behind her slow meandering; touching
what she touched, watching her face—more
distant with each feel;
her slight smile and unfocused eyes,
lost in cloth clairvoyance.

Ummmm, she would murmur
as she laid her hands upon each bolt,
three-buttoned tweed jacket;
rusched silk cowl neck;
pencil skirt with back kick-pleats . . .

TEQUILA POETRY FORM
(2-2-4-3)

i think
maybe
i just might be
hung-over

SIN

Who
could deny
themselves
the Muse
who comes,
singing;

violets
in her hair.

SCIENTIFIC PROOF THAT LOVE
MAKES THE WORLD GO ROUND

I always *knew* Orion was a male—
wide shoulders and heels;
three slim stars of waist;
the manly package.

It was years before I learned his package
was actually his *sword.*

But at the McDonald Observatory,
the telescope *proved* my theory—
revealing Orion's sword to be the nebula
where new stars are born.

Last night, his name fell from my lips
as you kissed me;
vertigo knocked stars
off their taut strings of existence;
meteors flailed through the sky.

And all the while, Creation
burst and flared;
the thin seeds of love
still the urgent birth of all things.

SEASONS

Maybe we are misinterpreting the Seasons.

Maybe a *good* Summer, to Summer,
is one where he rips open his shirt,
buttons flinging down across
his dark equator of ribs,
like meteors;
earth scalded by his gilded chest.

Maybe that's the goal of Summer—
all his strength wielded in solar testosterone
to make us crack and beg;
to singe the flesh down to bones.

And maybe a *good* Winter, to Winter,
is total white ice annihilation—
reaching her scissor-sharp toes
down into the mud of the Gulf,
the fish, flash-frozen mid swim.

Maybe it's their offspring we should
be wooing to stay longer—
chatty Spring, with her green highlights
and perky new breasts,

and her gay brother, Fall,
in his pumpkin turtleneck.
Fall, the sensitive poet
contemplating longer nights;
sharpened turkey quills in hand;

leaves falling as he shakes
his golden hair from his eyes.

GOD BLESS AMERICA

She said *everything* was better
in *her* country,
especially the food—
the eggs, for example.

In America, she said,
you eat unfertilized eggs,
but in *her* country,

they prefer the fertilized ones;
the crunch of tiny bones.

NO GIVE

He was angry, having learned
something about her from their
neighbour. But the truth was, in every way
but marriage, she

wasn't his anymore. Six
years before, that last word, rock
hard; wedged into the gap beside her heart,
forcing her taut;

fencepost straight. He looks out on
all he owns; tests the give of
tight barbed wires with his finger; smiles at his
own bloody gash.

DAWN OF A NATION

I have often looked at that behind the president without being able to tell whether it was rising or setting. But now I know that it is a rising sun.
    —Ben Franklin (after signing the US Constitution) commenting on the sun painting on George Washington's chair

It's said, in that moment, he *wept*—
wept for this wild land
carved by backbone and hatchet;

for a people bursting for freedom
like ripe Indian corn—*independence,*
rasped like flint upon their lips—

We the People;
We the People . . .
For three months they met,

hands striking and re-striking desks;
voices raised; delegates in full regalia
of stockings and weskits and wigs;

all gathered around the fire of inspired minds,
the swirl of feather; the scoot of chair; then it is
    done;
the sun always, *always* on the rise.

BEN FRANKLIN

He's been called the Patron Saint of American
    Printers,
the 15th out of 17 siblings;
the man who founded the American Philosophical
    Society;
who watched sparks tight rope down a kite string
to a dangling key,
declaring electricity may *help to make a vain man
humble.*

Perhaps he should be canonized, like St. Augustine,
who was told by a voice *tolle; lege* (Latin for *take
up and read*);
St Augustine, the patron saint of brewers and
    printers;
of sore eyes and theologians.

I've read Franklin's letters;
walked his cobblestone footsteps;
sat in his pew—number 70 in Christ's Church.
Every tough decision in my life, I've thought of him,
using his *Moral Algebra*—his Pro and Con list
of logical decision making.

And in April of 1773, he took a moment
to think forward,
wishing to invent a method
*of embalming drowned persons,
that they might be recalled to life
at any period, however distant,*
when three drowned flies poured out
of a newly opened bottle of Madeira wine.

He gently gathered them, and put them in the sun.
Hours later, two began to move,
wiped their eyes with their fore feet,
brushed their wings with their hind feet,
then flew away.

And he wished for himself, such suspension—
that he could wake to see America in 100 years.

To you, Saint Franklin, we raise a glass,
223 years later,
immersed in philosophy; poetry.
Let us die such an ordinary death;
our last thoughts of wine; of beauty;
of a land we have loved so well.

I thank you God for this most amazing day, for the leaping greenly spirits of trees, and for the blue dream of sky and for everything which is natural, which is infinite, which is yes.

—e.e. cummings

NICOLE

I never knew why he was so hard on us
until I met *her*, his only child,
with her exotic almond green eyes,
and a rebel streak stemming

from his ex's no discipline policy.
Living in that stair-step year
between my brother and myself,
we refused to let her in,

and her antics grew—stealing
my bicycle, trading it for bus tickets.
Each year, we'd load up in some bizarre
family gathering to fetch her,

the last time from an apartment across town.
They came out of it together,
Dad shaking his right, swollen fist . . .
That was the last summer we ever saw her,

her mother only calling once more,
the day after her funeral,
to tell him
his only daughter was dead.

GOD IN THE BATHTUB

God Says Yes to Me

—Kaylin Haught

Sometimes when I light candles,
God steps into the room, an aged
whiskey in one hand, tight cigar in the other.
Sometimes He joins me in the bath,

stretching His handsome, narrow feet
and long toes out next to mine.
Last night, I asked how He could be
in my tub *and* all over the world

at the same time. He said that was
the Holy Ghost thing—covering
the whole earth in the same moment
like a veil of smoke.

I asked if He created humans because
He was lonely. "Beauty," He answered
with some wise bath pearl Proverb,
"was *always* meant to be shared."

After a while in the silence and the warmth
I asked if *after* He made the earth and the beasts
and mankind, if He *still* ever got lonely. He paused
for a moment, like my husband used to do,

using the long drag of tobacco to articulate
heavy thoughts. "Yea," He said, leaning
back, closing those great grey eyes,
"*that* kind of lonely is the worst."

TWELVE STITCHES

Even the balsamic taste of caprese
can take me back to that day before Easter,
my brother and I colouring eggs;

Dad's temper flaring in the next room;
summoning Jesus with every failed
attempt of engine restoration.

Ah . . . *the holidays*—those holy days of
togetherness, rushing to the hospital from
flying steel parts; my brother's stigmata—

blood on his hands; his head;
one stitch for every year of his life.
And my father at the wheel,

still calling out to the Lord,
blessings on the blood, the traffic;
the Craftsman tools.

REFERENCE MATERIAL

He bought the book for its inscription
at the re-sell store, the handwritten note
from one lover to the other, declaring
eternal devotion: *In your quiet moments,*
may you always remember our love.

At home he placed it on the shelf,
next to the dictionary, thesaurus,
and the book about Pompeii, where
on page 36, a photo is earmarked—
a skeleton trapped in a house

on August 24, 79;
with only hours to live, suffocating
from the falling Vesuvius ash, he had
scratched into the beautifully frescoed wall:
Nothing in this world can endure forever.

SHAMELESS LOVE POEM

You, my love, are the perfect evening,
arms outstretched to balance

the tumbling sun in one hand,
the cool moon in the other;

you, the giver of light to the world.
And when you come home,

your brow ridged with work,
iridescence spins about your face,

stardust lingers in the crease of your wrists,
the crescent beds beneath your nails.

And still you reach for me,
enough shimmer left

to light the doorway, the room,
the dark space between my lips.

MY MOMENT OF AMERICA

for my brother, General Richard Martin

Years before, he swore he'd never eject,
said the rigors of losing a 14 billion dollar
airplane could outweigh survival.
But he changed his mind

300 feet off the ground,
his F-16 nose-diving into
the Turkish desert,
and pulled that lever—

a rocket beneath his seat;
his country in his heart;
God in his parachute,
and walked away.

That was *my* moment of America,
to realize flesh and blood—
my flesh and blood—would gladly
give his life; willingly stand before

the snarl of death . . . And each time I hear
that Star-Spangled Banner play,
I think of him there,
his grin beckoning *Come and Take It*;

behind him, the rocket's red glare.

PANGAEA

In the beginning, the world was bed,
and we clumped together,
a dark mass
in the middle of a white ocean.

But years of current and ice-age and quake
pushed between,
separating breasts from backs,
legs like long islands;

pillows filling curved gulfs;
continental drifts tilting us
to the polar ends of this flat,
square world with international waters;

and we became our own country—
with our own language;
each speaking in a way
the other cannot understand.

PARIS AS I SEE IT

for Elise Pierce

She said what she loves about Paris
are *the possibilities*;
the way sunrise smells
like warm croissants,

and midnight smells like pizza.
How morning stirs the colours in the Seine,
and people prefer formal grammar,
yet *french* in full view on the Metro;

how apartments are ranked
Haussmann and postwar;
how dogs are everywhere
but children rarely seen;

how current events take second
to pure butter, roasted chicken
and chocolate crepes;
how champagne comes before the wine;

and the locals smile as she butchers
the language, because that's *exactly*
how they like it—rich and tough,
but *perfect* with a nice bottle of red.

GIFT BASKET

I sent a gift basket
to your hotel room tonight.
I can imagine it there,
waiting patiently on the table.
I can see you,
coming in from your long flight,
eyeing the basket in the dim lights;
setting down the room key;
picking up my note; smiling.

I see you open the cellophane,
inhaling the scent of pears and pistachios,
ham and gouda;
touching the prize: the fragile fifth of whiskey.

What you can't see is in my mind . . .
for I'm there right now,
sitting in the middle of that dark mahogany table—
one knee curled underneath me,
the other pulled up to my chest.
It's *me* in there,
the heady scent of perfume and woman,
waiting *im*patiently
for you to touch your prize.

Cellophane grows warm against bare skin.

CALL ME BABY,

call me Lover,
call me Milady, Sister, Daughter,
Mother.
Call me Student; Escritor.
Call me Dreamer, Dancer,
Double-Dare Taker,
Poet.

Do not call me orphan,
widow, survivor,
amputee.

Let love fill these empty cavities
like stars in the dark;
making molds of missing parts,
torn dreams,
stomped hearts.

Let my soul walk whole.

Call me in your ecstasy;
your fingers in my hair;
in your gasp of shooting star;
call me, maybe,
Sexy Lady;
Sweet Jesus
Baby Baby, oh Baby.

WHY I MARRIED MY HUSBAND

Mother's three steadfast rules:

* You'll never get a man unless you can make good gravy.
* Never let a man take naked pictures of you, no matter what kind of art he calls it.
* Never trust a man who says 'trust me'.

Home for the summer from college,
I worked at the hospital, met this handsome boy—
reckless and worldly; far older than his age.

Our first date out, I climbed into his
spotless green Gran Torino
with shiny rims and glass packs,
and he told me our plans—
to meet his friends for Happy Hour.

But I wasn't sure, had never had a drink before.
I don't know . . . can I trust you?

He looked me up and down,
slammed that racer into gear,
back tires whipping out of the parking lot
"Hell No".

It's easier to leap if you're already dancing.
                                                        —Rain Bojangles

ANNIVERSARY AT SEA

I cannot think of things so grand.
I cannot wrap my thoughts around

concepts like eternity, or
double cousins, or dethroned saints,

or rainfall in the Pantheon,
or how sea turtles hold their breath,

or the depth of Fate's tentacles—
how a lifetime of miracles

could sync into that one moment
when two separate lives would meet.

But see this horizon, my love,
this perfect vision each soul craves;

this sea, this seamless line of blue,
is but a million tiny waves.

FOR ALL THINGS, GREAT AND SMALL

I have not yet sat and lingered
in this chair—
this chair upstairs,
claimed by my daughter;

and I look out the window
to see her view.

She needs a lamp here,
and a tiny side table.

And there, in those bushes
by the bridge,
she needs some flowers.

I won't tell her I planted bulbs
this fall,

that she might look from
this very spot next spring,
and a marvel at the daffodils
and hyacinth and paper whites,

and think to herself
how glorious this life;

how even the flowers
seem to bloom
just for her.

HER NIGHT EYES

One hour after sunset, I paced
while she dressed
and powdered her face,
and darkened the abyss
of her eyes;

then gasped as I saw her
piercing the threshold of my earth,
hand on hip,
posing for the cameras
of my eyes;

and the black anger scatted back
to my shadow,
impatience vanished like fog from
the spell of her,

the blossom,
damp,
cool
smell of her.

Oh you, the Moon
of my night,
take my skin; let's slip
a little sin in our sway;

you who *electrify* the stars
of the night;
let us heed the primal pull
let's *go forth and multiply.*

LEAP YEAR

for Fred and Kay Campbell, Keepers of Paint Rock

I didn't ask about Leap Year,
standing among pictographs drawn
12,000 years ago in Paint Rock;
pictographs so precise, that at 12:35 p.m.
every Winter Equinox,
a spear of light points into a drawn eye,
then becomes a light ladder
another drawn figure walks up.

They marked equinoxes, solstices, lunar events—
they who worshipped the creator of the sun
and the moon and the stars.

Yet, we call them *primitive*—a nomadic people
thriving 10,000 years before Christ was even *born*—

the first writers; first storytellers; their teachings
still awaiting our eyes from stacked bluff walls.
They, *of course*, would have *known* about
this subtle gain of time.

Maybe it's the magic we felt
when we stopped outside Cross Plains,
and leaned against each other in the night;
a magic four years coming,

when we learned
nothing is random in this universe;
that every 15 minutes we've shared
led to that night;

to that extra gift of hours
under ancient stars—
their lights like tiny arrows
in our eyes.

CATTAILS

You, whom I could not save. —Czeslaw Milosz

Suddenly I realize that if I stepped out of my body
I would break into blossom. —James Wright

Two days after you jumped,
    you whom I could not save,
I saw a cloud in the sky—
arms spread in flight,
body angled downward.

To you,
    the man I could not save;
    the man I did not know;
    the man I never met;
I hope in your last moments
you smiled;
the wind *perfect* beneath your palms
as you soared 800 feet down;
the brilliant March sun
bursting every cattail in the Gorge.

STREET CORNERS

It's been our monthly battle for 25 years:
money.
Hard earned by him,
too easily given away by me.

A man of structure, he has a method
of spending, of tithing,
giving a big part of his salary to charity.

Yet still, I can't help but give more.
I buy from every child at the door,
remembering the time when dreams
were something you slept with every night;
what you lived for every day.

I look at haggard beggars on the street corners,
but all I can see are dusty-headed boys,
heads thrown back as they swing;
toes high in the air—
pointed up to the man they couldn't wait to become.

JOY

for Margaret Chalfant

I have opened myself
to wonder;
allowed joy
to flood into my life
every day.
I've witnessed
a creek's current
turning upstream;
and hawks upon my gate.
I've been brought to tears
by desert plains,
full moons and newborn calves;
by snow dusting off tree limbs;
by hot running bath water.
And just last week,
a horse-apple
fell to the sidewalk
beside us at lunch.
I can't tell you how often
I've thought of that dimpled
green ball—its thump and roll,
or our surprise and laughter.
Maybe God
likes us to expect Him
this close.
Maybe happiness
is just that easy.

LEGEND OF THE ASPEN:
THE CHRYSOPOEIA*

Years later, they would look at those mountains,
in the Sangre de Cristo forest,
and see where the lovers had traveled.

Bits of wild, brilliant yellow
clearly marked each moment
they thought of one another;
or when the wind carried the scent of her hair
to his face;
or when their arms brushed,
as he lifted a hanging branch from her path.

This was *the* love;
the love that made the gods wish for mortality;
the love men lived and died for,
the love that transformed the world.

Alchemist steam
streamed and rippled, and curled from their bodies
in the cool mountain air,
turning the trees in the heat of their wake;
ripening each tender green Aspen leaf,
until they blushed,
radiant and golden—
as though Midas, himself
breathed morning blessings in the fog.

* chrysopoeia—the transmutation into gold

A LITTLE FLOWER

"Just living is not enough," said the Butterfly, *"one must have sunshine, freedom, and a little flower."*
— Hans Christian Anderson

Sunbathing beneath the pear tree,
her lime green leaves flirting
in front of jealous oaks,
she called me outside;
the early warmth, an invitation
to shed my fleece and jeans and socks
down to a camisole and yellow panties;
white flowers falling on my skin
like scented spring snow.

I was told not to plant her—
her life, frail and fast;
but *she* is the brazen one—
the first bud, first blossom,
first plaything of the wind,
first desire of young bees;
laughing as winter beats his chest;
the girl with the longest summer;
her ruffling skirts of green.

ABOUT THE AUTHOR

karla k. morton, the 2010 Texas Poet Laureate, is a Councilor of the Texas Institute of Letters and a graduate of Texas A&M University. Described as "one of the most adventurous voices in American poetry," she is a Betsy Colquitt Award Winner, twice an Indie National Book Award Winner, the recipient of the Writer-in-Residency E2C Award in Seaside, Florida, and the author of nine collections of poetry. Morton has been twice nominated for the Pushcart Prize, is a nominee for the National Cowgirl Hall of Fame, and established an ekphrastic collaborative touring exhibit titled: *No End of Vision: Texas as Seen By Two Laureates*, pairing photography with poetry with Texas Poet Laureate Alan Birkelbach. Morton's work has been used by many students in their UIL Contemporary Poetry contests, and was recently featured with seven other prominent authors in *8 Voices: Contemporary Poetry of the American Southwest*.